02 5082240

BC-3

CL

THE EVERGLADES

NATURAL WONDERS

Jason Cooper

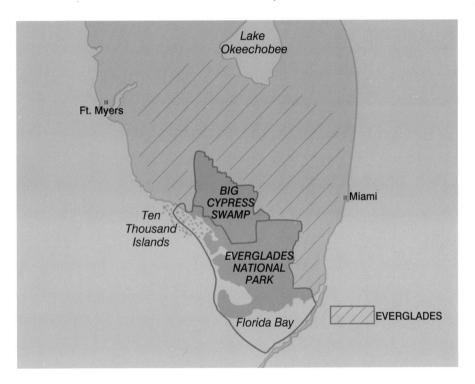

The Rourke Press, Inc.
Vero Beach, Florida 32964

© 1995 The Rourke Press, Inc.

PHOTO CREDITS
All photos © Lynn M. Stone

Library of Congress Cataloging-in-Publication Data

Cooper, Jason, 1942-
   The Everglades / Jason Cooper
      p. cm. — (Natural Wonders)
   Includes index.
   ISBN 1-57103-017-4
   1. Everglades (Fla.)—Juvenile literature.   2. Everglades National
Park (Fla.)—Juvenile literature.   I. Title II. Series
F317.E9C66 1995
917.59' 39—dc20

                                      95–12303
                                         CIP
                                         AC

Printed in the USA

TABLE OF CONTENTS

THE EVERGLADES

The Everglades is a huge, wet wilderness in south Florida. It is a mix of swamps, marshes, ponds, rivers, forests, and wide, wet **prairies** (PRAR reez).

This great wetland is a home for more than 900 **species** (SPEE sheez), or kinds, of plants and 600 species of animals—without counting insects.

The Everglades region was once the size of Massachusetts and Connecticut. Much of the 'glades has been drained, however. Today it is about half its former size.

Sawgrass prairie and tree hammocks cover much of the Everglades

THE EVERGLADES RIVER

Southern Florida is like a slightly tilted saucer. Water from Lake Okeechobee and the Kissimmee River used to flow southward through the Everglades to Florida Bay and the ocean. The sheet of fresh water was a wide, shallow river.

Water still flows through the 'glades, but not in the same way that nature planned. Canals and other water control structures have changed the way the 'glades take a drink.

During the wet season, a shallow river flows south through sawgrass prairies and over the ragged limestone rock bottom of the 'glades

PLANTS

The Everglades has many communities of plants. The depth of water and the height of land help decide which plants root.

Sawgrass grows throughout much of the Everglades "river." The rough edges of sawgrass cut flesh like a saw.

Pines, palms, and several hardwood trees grow in the driest part of the 'glades. Bays, cypresses, and mangroves grow in wet places. Spidery air plants and orchids clasp tree branches and trunks.

Water-and-fire resistant pines grow on some   9
   of the higher ground of the Everglades

ANIMALS

Great flocks of long-legged wading birds live in the Everglades. Bald eagles, ospreys, pelicans and about 275 other species of birds live in the 'glades, too.

The 'glades are home for water-loving critters—otters, alligators, crocodiles, turtles, fish, and snakes. The rare Florida panther lives mostly in the nearby Big Cypress Swamp.

A colorful land snail lives in the branches of tree islands called **hammocks** (HAM ehks).

A roseate spoonbill, brightest of the Everglades wading birds, flashes pink

The number of endangered wood storks (shown here) and other wading birds has dropped sharply with changes to the Everglades

The mangrove-covered Ten Thousand Islands (seen here from the air) make up the western edge of Everglades National Park

WONDERS OF THE EVERGLADES

Nowhere else in the world is there a great sea of sawgrass like that in the Everglades. Nowhere else are there such large forests of red mangrove trees. The creeks that thread through the mangroves are great for canoe adventures.

For most visitors, the wild animals are the real wonders. Visitors especially love alligators, pelicans, and the pink spoonbills.

Alligators live throughout the Everglades region where they hunt fish, turtles, and even smaller alligators

SEASONS

Like the world's tropical places, the Everglades has basically two seasons. It has a wet summer season, usually from June into October. It has a dry winter season from October through May.

Summer is hot, buggy, and humid. Thunderstorms crackle. Hard, almost-daily rains soak the 'glades.

Winter is cooler. Water is scarce, so animals collect at ponds and deep water channels called **sloughs** (SLOOZ).

Summer rains help fill Everglades ponds to the brim

PEOPLE IN THE 'GLADES

People first reached the Everglades about 3,000 years ago. They lived in the hammocks, and ate shellfish and wild plants and animals.

In the 1800's, Miccosukee and Seminole people moved into the 'glades. Many of these Native Americans still live in the Everglades region.

People began projects to drain water from the Everglades in 1881. Those projects continued into the 1970's. The 'glades were drained so that former wetlands could be used for towns and farms.

A water truck showers a tomato crop ripening in a field that was part of the Everglades until it was drained

EVERGLADES NATIONAL PARK

Not everyone wanted to make south Florida's wet land dry. In 1947, the U.S. Government created Everglades National Park.

Today the park's 1,500,000 acres protect much of the remaining Everglades and its wildlife. It is the third largest national park outside Alaska. The nearby Big Cypress National Preserve also protects Everglades animals and is a source of Everglades water.

Fifteen species of animals in the park are in danger of becoming **extinct** (ex TINGKT)—gone forever. Unfortunately, the park itself is in danger, too.

White pelicans glide at dawn across Florida Bay in Everglades National Park

THE EVERGLADES TOMORROW

Everglades National Park should be safe, but its plants, animals, and water quality are suffering.

Huge canals, dikes, ponds, and pipes control the flow of much of the surface water to the park. The amount of water reaching the park is often too little—or too much. Water does not always reach the park when it is needed—another problem.

Several government efforts are under way to help bring a more natural water flow to the park. In time, perhaps they will succeed.

Glossary

extinct (ex TINGKT) — to have disappeared altogether as a living species

hammock (HAM ehk) — an island of trees usually surrounded by lower, wetter land

prairies (PRAR reez) — treeless, grassy areas either damp or dry; grasslands

sloughs (SLOOZ) — long, deep pools or channels of water in a wetland

species (SPEE sheez) — a certain kind of animal within a closely related group; for example, a *roseate* spoonbill

INDEX